The Rest of the Way

poems by

Tom Laughlin

Finishing Line Press
Georgetown, Kentucky

The Rest of the Way

Copyright © 2022 by Tom Laughlin
ISBN 978-1-64662-918-3 First Edition
All rights reserved under International and Pan-American Copyright Conventions. No part of this book may be reproduced in any manner whatsoever without written permission from the publisher, except in the case of brief quotations embodied in critical articles and reviews.

ACKNOWLEDGMENTS

Grateful acknowledgement is made to the editors of the publications in which the following poems first appeared, sometimes in slightly different forms:

Blue Mountain Review: "Jazz"
Dead River Review: "Finally Beyond the Pine-Treed Back Roads of my Morning Commute, I Think of You Early This September Morning"
Drunk Monkeys: "Hurrying Home to My Father"
Grey Sparrow Journal: "Turning Home"
Howth Castle: "The Rest of the Way"
Ibbetson Street: "Disillusionment of January Tenth," "James Wright's Hammock," and "Monday Morning on the Town Green"
Middlesex Magazine: "Hindsight"
Molecule: "March 2nd, 70°"
Muddy River Poetry Review: "Before the Fourth Nor'easter" and "Night Swimming at Lake Waban"
North Essex Review: "Early Lessons" and "Flame Thrower"
Rockvale Review: "Along Tornado Alley"
Sand Hills Literary Magazine: "Dendrophile" and "The Late-Summer Day"
The Somerville Times: "Mistress"
Superpresent Magazine: "Father's Lessons"
Vortext: "Unsunday"

Publisher: Leah Huete de Maines
Editor: Christen Kincaid
Cover Photo: Tom Laughlin
Author Photo: Ranjoo Herr
Cover Design: Elizabeth Maines McCleavy

Order online: www.finishinglinepress.com
also available on amazon.com

Author inquiries and mail orders:
Finishing Line Press
PO Box 1626
Georgetown, Kentucky 40324
USA

Table of Contents

Early Lessons 1

Flame Thrower 2

Jazz 3

Turning Home 5

Along Tornado Alley 6

Elements 7

The Rest of the Way 8

James Wright's Hammock 10

March 2nd, 70° 11

Mistress 12

Disillusionment of January Tenth 13

Hindsight 15

Dendrophile 16

Hurrying Home to My Father 18

Great White 19

The Late-Summer Day 20

Unsunday 22

Monday Morning on the Town Green 23

Finally Beyond the Pine-Treed Back Roads of my Morning Commute, I Think of You Early this September Morning 25

Father's Lessons 26

Before the Fourth Nor'easter 28

Night Swimming at Lake Waban 30

With Thanks 31

for Miya and Peg

Early Lessons

I remember a pig
chewing on the back of
a live chicken
on a farm when I was fourteen.

Kicked out of its coop at midday
by my pitchfork scraping the crusty floor,
the chicken climbed into the pig stall
looking for shade from the yard's burning heat.

Paddy came quickly, the dogs barking behind,
following my frantic sprint,
to grab the still blinking chicken
from grunting snouts.

"Too far gone," he spun it by the neck,
then held it out
to flutter, jerk,
then hang limp from his hand.

Flame Thrower

A lefty,
the guns weren't made for him
so he became a flame thrower:
flushing out fox holes that
couldn't be cleared.

Children on fire
still rip through his dreams,
forcing him down to the kitchen chair
at three in the morning
for a cigarette, high-ball, and late movie.

I knew only hatred
standing below that bald, leather head,
slapped in the face
by the crooked fingers
of his open hand.

Dead buddies...malaria...
teeth knocked in, words
shouted into arguments too often
to cut deeply when intended,
burn years later for a flame-thrower's son.

Jazz

dancing boy, danc-
          ing girl
and a boy   again
tiptoeing on the wooden raft
circling as it sways
he circles and it sways in the stillness
of the creek
around and to the diving
board where he rattles and thumps and springs
                twirling float-
                          ing up and out
and curving down to slice
then splash
          then explode up
and out splashing shouting laughing at the moon
swirling in the hot summer dusk
thrashing and kicking with smiling wetness
     before climbing the ladder to sit back
smile
and watch to see the girl
tip-toe on the swaying dock
circle
no not circle
        almost circle to the edge
then almost circle again
as the creek stills
        ripples slightly anticipation
        her footsteps
pat the dampened wood
     she finds
        the worn wooden board—
bobs up, rattles rattles and slaps running to take that board
bending, spring-   ing as part of her
          part of the swing of her arms soaring upward
the slow subtle arc and twist of her naked shoulders outward

                              twirling floating

                                                            flying
outward and down slicing unexpectedly, swallowing
her reflection, toes pointing to the last
the aching unruffling pause
before
exploding up smiling, laughing to herself, to the raft, to
that hot-mooned dusky August day

and she turns splashing, suddenly racing, toward
              the reaching-branched shore tree
       the boy now unfolds his sitting to sprint
thumping and springing out quickly over creek water
spraying strokes pushing in pursuit of the laughing hair
reaching toward the rooted wild-grassed bank

she grabs the knot-
ted rope past the thick trunk, up
the dirt path to
       pausing
              deep-breathed jump
                     holding hanging swish-
ing beyond trunk and path
whistling wildly over grassy bank
                            then water
then over the boy
              half out of the creek, caught
in a broadening smile of awe
              and appreciation, watching
the arcing girl as she sails
then dances on her smooth-watered reflection

Turning Home

These hills have echoed in my ears
for decades
boulder-flecked peaks rattling my windy thoughts
treed birds chirping me higher

I have smelled these fields through my shoulders
wherever I pause
sun-drenched blades rippling for wind
rasping every movement
tickling my muscles with hot greenness

These horses have grazed my chest
—even now, through frosted-crisp December air
tails waving hypnotic symphonies
nostril snorts filling my lungs

This lake has burrowed into my bones
lapping steadily under skin
sky reflecting through turtled fingers
swallowing my muddy darkness

These woods have crackled my feet
at every step
oaked messages whispering into soles
hidden twigs laughing between toes
pine tops sprouting through my skull

Along Tornado Alley

"The power's out—I'm going to bed"
he says and heads up
the worn wooden staircase
that fourth step still creaking
railing loose at the top.

After eighty years in Wichita
he's grown used to twisters
sirens
warnings on the radio.
Sometimes you know they're coming
sometimes not.

He's seen roofs ripped off
houses shredded like tissue paper
fence posts speared into oak trees
and friends
or what remained of them.
He'd been taught in school how to run
to storm cellars, brace himself in
door frames, pray.

In total darkness tonight
he strips to his boxers
says goodnight to photos on the wall
feels the lack of weight at the foot of the bed
while reciting his nighttime prayer
and reaching to touch the cold pillow beside him.
He listens to rain pummeling the clapboards
howling winds rattling a pane in need of puttying
and waits for sleep.

Elements

The winds picked up every time we made plans
rain swirling sideways and pounding streets
opening coats, soaking pantlegs socks shoes
umbrellas useless each night as we leaned
winded, tossed right then left
splashing toward restaurant, sports bar, billiard hall.

We shook hair and draped dripping coats
laughed tentatively over soggy
clothes attempting to dry under
tablecloth or barstool.

Still the storm raged, wind and hail
waiting outside for our attempts to reach
car, train, coffee shop, apartment.
In time our forced laughter was no match
for the forces darkening our every meeting
leaving forecasters dumbstruck.

Reduced to the rawness of telephones
dampened conversations where
dreams of clear-skied lilac scented strolls
remained unspoken, our connections
grew hazier, the line crackling with snow
until our final trailing off
into a puddle of silence.

The Rest of the Way

Start here
just beyond the chain fence
on the back street
it turns to footpath
ahead, then left along
the water. There's
wild grass and seagulls
and the path breaks
down into dirt
around a boarded-up
pumphouse. Look at
the islands out away
and bridge connecting
two with the mainland.
The dock by that white
house there has boats
sometimes, visitors.
Breathe in seaweed
even dead fish smells
but don't stop—round
that corner the city large across
the bay, above the beach
where old men swim naked
every day—even through winter.
The steps of stone are wide
but low. They curve
too, like a rising
tunnel pulling you
to street and long-
needled spruce that reach
asking for the brush
of a hand
passing. Down the slope

past the field that fills
with pheasants in spring
go right
and you'll recognize
the rest of the way.

James Wright's Hammock

Empty,
It rocks slightly
In the imperceptible mid-summer breeze,
The once white rope bronzed by sun and rain, frayed.
Midday rays slowly scorch
The tall grass gone to seed,
A pair of silent scrub pines
Re-measuring seven gray field stones
Between them. Fence post remnants
Slide into the ravine.
From a dusty corner nest
In the Duffys' abandoned barn,
A swallow swoops its sickle-like wings,
Snatches a butterfly in flight,
Orange disappearing
As quickly as it arrived.
This is where I wake.

March 2nd, 70°

Suddenly whistle-smile warmth
opening over snow drifts
releasing t-shirt Frisbee topped students
to open windowed hair in the breeze
orange school busses speeding homeward
cellared bicycles climbing bulkhead steps
skateboard kicking teens carving up Main Street.

Inside, those of us clocked
and tied in offices
feel sap rising
our smiles stretching out like limbs.

Mistress

she arrives quietly every month
catching me unaware
outside my office door
dusk quickly spreading on my way to car, home
the sight of her distracts me
the night's air warm and musky
damp from a week's ground-soaking rain

my car, too, conspires
finds the too-familiar darkened lot
my footsteps soundless, fearful
feeling now toward the concealed path
the gnarled protection of ancient limbs
long versed in such escapades
smiling at these pungent urges

as I climb steadily
pulse throbbing at my temples
she whispers through the pines
winking suggestively between splayed branches
behind, beside
around the distant beyond of
this great dark hill

so I find myself here again
atop a craggy-faced rock
gazing at her naked glory
bright and unabashed
ever the tease, hovering beside Orion's belt
and laughing now
with this pale and hungry lunatic

Disillusionment of January Tenth

Spent Christmas trees lie naked on sidewalks
embarrassed, unable to stand
their sappy stumps exposed, skirtless now, frozen
phantom roots no longer twitching toward
soil a branch-length away from their asphalt slabs

Beyond the closed front doors
colored lights flicker only from flat screens
onto winter-paled faces of couched men
their women binge-watching in kitchens
offspring shooting car thieves or texting catfish in separate rooms

The town beach lot has been empty since summer
a ball of dirty snow the only thing parked now
in a shady corner
metal signed warnings askew
on the chain linked gate

The full-bellied lake is still in watery motion
a child's jostled bucket of blue green
sprinkled here and there with white foam
shards of yellow sun
gentle palms of wind sweeping the surface

Where lake meets crusted sand
fall leaves have tangled themselves
into frosted clumps, a splayed brown line
ice-manacled in their final attempt
to return home

The wind-chilled beach ends
at a small, unkempt cove
where a boat dock sticks out its long tongue
laughing at the crooked remnants of an old stone retaining wall
and overgrown banks holding back hills of dark earth and trees

The shallow, protected cove is topped with a layer of ice
thinned to wine glass
along a curved edge
but resolute in its efforts to stand firm
against the clumsy hands of open water

While dozens of its watery trinkets
floating fragments of delicate ice
roll together with each rippling wave
tinkle and jingle rhythmically
against the cove's glassy ceiling

The ethereal sounds resonating out
along that crystal instrument
like winter wind chimes
or the distant bells
of a magical sleigh

Hindsight

I should have watched you
dance with hips and eyes
sliding in and out over
white then red lights
repeating moves you
saw I liked your lips open-
mouthing the words into
my eyes following as
hips roll together
circling and lower
bodies parallel with back
to front and back for
breaths close, chests brush

                    then quickly the head whips
                    away hair streaming across
                    sideward eyes, hinted smile
                    shoulders dancing

suddenly with themselves.

Dendrophile

They were our jungle gyms
our hanging bars
our hobby horses
our August cooling tents
our winter snow shakers
our climbing walls
our mountain tops
our citadels.

They surrounded us
as we ran chasing each other
past their sappy bark
over pine-needle thickened paths
the forest floor squishy with mulch
and the fibrous, reaching roots
of these silent sentinels standing watch
over our boyhood selves
as we grabbed for sticks at our feet—
broken branches weakened by boring insects
chiseled by birds bashing their hungry heads
and cracked loose by the weight of winter—
swinging and slamming these against trunks
snapping pieces that spun in the air
flying past ecstatic eyes
and nearly clipping our crew-cutted heads.

And whose six-year-old challenge was it
that day which set us attempting to climb
pole-thin pines
with their pencil pointed stubs
of branches long choked off
by the thick canopy of green high above?
Grabbing scratchy trunks
we stepped carefully, slowly
easing our weight onto

one bone-dry stub
then another
the height competition continuing
until a brittle crack to suddenly drop us
tumbling to pine-needled floor.

Then, unthinking
my sights on bragging rights
I reached up one stubbled trunk
hugging too closely its scratchy bark
as I climbed
until the crack
the sudden drop
the unseen sharpened stub
slicing
as I pole-slid toward forest floor
a thin red line
from my belly to chest.

Afterwards
the stitches
the bandages
the long torso scar
were show and tell exhibits
until puberty and chest hair
and decades erased
any visible sign
of that first woodland infection
when sap began
running through my veins.

Hurrying Home to My Father

A purple moon reaches
suddenly out from within
thick trees, finding branches
weakened by October's shake
while the highway weaves
and sinks. Jumping

above the trees
after a winding left,
it's orange this time
and staring—unround—
until a wall of truck
rushes by, forcing my eyes
back to the road.

Yellow now and higher
on this straight stretch,
it moves as strangely
as you—wheeled home
the last time, your left hand
grasping for my right.

My headlights, alone
follow the exit
into the wooded street
I bicycled years earlier.
Home is ahead
where trees close in
on the narrowing road.

Great White

I know motion
Moving is what I do
Like the depths of blue-green
Dancing scents along my smooth sides
Teasing this gnawing
Within my belly
There is never choice, only motion
Desire
And scents that pull me faster
The ecstasy of conquest
—a union of sorts
Of life and blood
Pungent taste of flesh

And yet the hunger returns
Again and again
The search
The motion

At times I have resisted, waited
Ignored the pangs
Watched as others partook
Felt disgust at the sight

Yet there is pride in this jaw, these teeth
And what I am built for in this world
Strength, speed, and even a grace of sorts
Though few see this in me

The Late-Summer Day
for Mary Oliver

Halfway across Walden Pond
the mid-September sun bright above the tree-line
reflects off the smooth surface
and warms my squinting face as I swim,
my hands reaching gently through the clear water
of this late afternoon.
The thickness of woods along the shores
holds me in its arms
as I turn to swim back toward sandy shore
and the old wooden bathhouse basking in light
with a speckle of old swimmers and beach chair readers.
Floating in the water just ahead of me, a small stick
or piece of trash distracts me
until closer, I see the light green body,
the orange stripe, and the small legs
of a grasshopper, motionless. How did she get here
far out in the middle, with no grass or land in sight?
No boats today with a fisherman who may not have noticed
a quiet stow-away. And how have the trout, bass, and pickerel
missed this tasty morsel?
I reach to cup its body in one hand
water draining through my fingers
to see and feel the hair-like front legs
and feathery body
until it jumps   alive suddenly   How?
landing just ahead, back on the water.
I'm the only island in sight, I think
and slower this time, cup my hand and lift
gently carrying her toward the top of my head
where she steps on, clinging to my wet hair.
Holding my neck and head as still as possible on the long swim in,
I feel her move through my hair, climbing to higher ground perhaps
and I wonder what she sees from her perch
with those *enormous and complicated eyes*
and whether Mary Oliver ever carried a grasshopper on her head.

As my feet touch sand, my head rising with its passenger
I walk, slowly, out of the water, across the sand
past toweling swimmers and a curious child
up to the stone-walled ledge
where I bow my head to the thick blades of green beyond
feel the small snap of her back legs
and see her fling herself back into the grass.

Unsunday

Sunday gray day grumpy
we sit on the couch feeling the weight
of our bones, flesh, arms
not quite able to move the newspaper
sections or comforter twisted up
underneath unmoving legs, sweat-
panted and socked, a mile and three days away
from the coffee table, a half cup
now cold on top of Living/Arts.
Eyes glazed, hair matted, untalking,
unsure of what would feel enjoyable,
of what could be done in the waning hours of
this empty afternoon,
we become furniture, plants drooping
for lack of water, sun, dust coating
leaves that face floorward.
Even the clock has forgotten how to move.

Monday Morning on the Town Green

The old gazebo is alone
adrift in an empty emerald sea
longing for company again
on this blue-sky morning.
Protected from summer sun by its wide-brimmed hat
it hums a jazzy clarinet solo
still echoing from Saturday night's concert
which radiated in all directions, dancing out
across a rainbow of blankets, coolers, and picnicking families.

Set upon a cement mantelpiece
at the center of the green
six steps up from the neatly trimmed grass
it watches the last of the dew drying
four or five sleepy bees searching for clover
and waits for a Frisbee, Whiffle ball, or cross-legged reader.

A blonde, skirted and sandaled young mother exits
the superette across the street
squints both ways while
speaking gently to a small hand in each of hers
signaling with nods and a point of her chin
but turning left now to pass outside the north fence
eyes and soft words ahead to the day.

One of the small hands
has turned her pigtailed attention
bobbing sideways a moment
toward the mantled gazebo—
a playhouse on green carpet
a place for dragons and doggies
tongues hanging their welcomes out
over the white fenced railings
her green tickled toes giggling round

and round the open air castle—
before being pulled forward again
away from the infinite green of possibilities
from the now crestfallen gazebo and
back to the dry sand of the road's weary edges.

Finally Beyond the Pine-Treed Back Roads of my Morning Commute, I Think of You Early this September Morning

The bright sun kisses
The corn fields that I pass
Grown tall and stretched
Near to bursting
With plump kernels of sweetness within
Golden gems that sparkle and spill out over the tops
Yellow happiness
Dancing like fireworks
Against a green stalked sky

Because of you
I, too, feel these golden gems
This yellow happiness
This full heart bursting into dance

Father's Lessons

When asked a question,
respond with nonsense or irony

When someone sits alone at a party,
go chat with and help them feel welcome

When telling a story,
perform with voices, gestures, and silly faces

When a game or activity requires equipment,
improvise with an old broom, cardboard box, or ball of tape

When in a restaurant, store, movie theatre, or park,
speak to all strangers encountered

When listening to music or watching a remotely sentimental film,
cry

When sharing memories,
don't worry too much about the truth

When any distant cousin dies,
go to the wake, even if it's 120 miles away

When holiday dinner decorum is expected,
throw a roll across the table for a laugh

When tired or depressed,
pretend everything is fine

When asked about war service,
offer only rank and serial number

When it serves any small purpose,
lie

When the darkness of evening comes on,
drink

When arriving home late to wife and children,
drink, numb pain, attack others

When haunted by demons,
drink, numb pain, attack others

When bedtime finally comes,
pass out in a chair

When woken by nightmares in the small hours,
find a bottle, sit alone, try again to numb the pain

Before the Fourth Nor'easter

Today in the woods, the pine tops rest quietly
against an empty blue sky.
My booted steps follow
a jagged trough of a trail
left behind by skis and snow shoes,
their early-morning elves nowhere in sight now
and the distant chatter of chickadees and nuthatches
hushing suddenly when I approach
in a snowy conspiracy of silence.

In the blinding beauty of last week's storm,
buckled, booted, and hooded tightly,
I walked the center of empty streets,
stepping into snowbanks when plows passed,
the mile to my daughter's house
to be welcomed inside by her mother, grandmother
and leaping retriever, clearing snow-covered clothes
for tea and family talk. But my daughter,
too busy, stayed in her room.

Yesterday's news
from my daughter's high school
was of another "unexpected passing,"
the family not wanting to share details
the homeroom students gasping
at an empty chair
the sobbing from hallways
the red-eyed teachers
the unanswered questions.

My jagged snowy trail wanders
around downed trees, over nearly invisible foot bridges
past the bright white clearing of a vernal pool
and by late afternoon downward toward unfamiliar land.

As my usual return paths are buried beneath heavy snow
I follow the elfin trail through a thickening shade of pines
down a steep incline until the trail splits, then peters out.
So I'm plunging deep now with each step
determined to find my way back through these woods.

Night Swimming at Lake Waban

Nearly full dark now
the winding road ends
and I pull in to park in the dirt
before feeling the thick grass
my bare feet choose
beside the path
that curves around an ancient stone building.
Approaching the water, I smell pipe smoke
and know I will not be alone tonight.
The lake is still

and so too is the old pipe smoker
the stone he sits upon
and his fishing pole
pointing out over water's edge
the line disappearing into dusky light
and dark reflections.
I hear the New England accent as we greet
and start down irregular steps of stone
set carefully by fellow swimmers years ago.
"I hope I don't scare your fish," I say aloud.

Careful to avoid the invisible fishing line, I step slowly forward
deeper along rock then sandy bottom
the water welcoming and smooth
heading away from the fisherman's line
out now and out and out across the darkness.
"Scare the fish in to shore," he calls to me
from the pitch-black shore trees
I have left behind
to become a lone bobber
in a universe of stars.

With Thanks

I am deeply indebted to Jim Laughlin for his generous help with this manuscript and his encouragement, support, and insightful feedback over more than four decades.

I am grateful for all the support and helpful feedback from my current writing group, Elena Graceffa, Dan Junkins, Jim Laughlin, Sarah Laughlin, & Rick Waks; my previous writing group at Massasoit Community College, Joyce Rain Anderson, Claire Krasnow, Ed Krasnow, John Philibert, and Tim Trask; the students, faculty, and community members who attended weekly Creative Writing Hours at Massasoit and at Middlesex Community College; as well as the students in my creative writing classes at Middlesex Community College who continue to inspire me.

Many thanks to the following writing teachers, colleagues, and friends for their wisdom, insights, inspiration, and support: Martha Collins, Lloyd Schwartz, Carole Simmons Oles, Cornelia Veenendaal, T.J. Anderson III, Joe Torra, Mary Buchinger, Albert Desrochers, Bill Hammond, Richard E. Miller, Kirk Etherton, Lucy Holstedt, Phyllis Gleason, Ellen Nichols, Caryl Dundorf, Gail Mooney, Joe Nardoni, Jonathan Bennett Bonilla, Cathy McCarron, Jill Keller, Lynn Gregory, Lara Kradinova, Matthew Olson, Katie Durant, Willy Ramirez, Ranjoo Herr, Susan Farmer, Ed Jacobs, Albert Hutton, Auberta Jacobs, and the Heffernan clan.

Deep gratitude to my mother, Peg Laughlin, for introducing me to the power of the word, and to the extended family of poets she inspired, for their ongoing creativity, comradery, and support.

Love and thanks to Miya and Linda for their inspiration and enthusiastic support.

And thanks to Christen Kincaid, Leah Huete de Maines, and everyone at Finishing Line Press.

Tom Laughlin is a professor at Middlesex Community College in Massachusetts where he teaches creative writing, literature, and composition courses, as well as coordinating the MCC Visiting Writers Series and open readings and contests featuring students, faculty, staff, and community members for the Creative Writing Program. He was a founding editor of *Vortext*, a literary journal of Massasoit Community College, and a volunteer staff reader for many years for *Ploughshares*. He has also taught literature classes in two Massachusetts prisons. His poetry and fiction have appeared in *Green Mountains Review, Ibbetson Street, Drunk Monkeys, Sand Hills Literary Magazine, The Blue Mountain Review, Muddy River Poetry Review, North Essex Review, Middlesex Magazine, The Dead River Review, Grey Sparrow Journal, Superpresent Magazine, Rockvale Review, Molecule,* and elsewhere. He has also published academic articles in *Teaching English in the Two-Year College* and elsewhere, as well an annual calendar, *Stone Balancing at Walden Pond*, featuring photos of his stone balancing. An avid hiker, pond swimmer, and Ultimate Frisbee player, he lives in Framingham, Massachusetts. His website is www.TomLaughlinPoet.com

CPSIA information can be obtained
at www.ICGtesting.com
Printed in the USA
JSHW020630050822
28920JS00004B/19